Vegetables

and Other Relationships

Scott Wiggerman

Plain View Press
P. O. 33311
Austin, TX 78764

plainviewpress.com
e-mail: SBRIGHT1@austin.rr.com
1-800-878-3605

Acknowledgments

I gratefully acknowledge the following publications, which have published the following poems: @*austin*: "Asparagus," "Creation"; *Austin Writer*: "Lost and Found"; *Bay Windows*: "Breakfast," "Size Queen"; *Black Buzzard Review*: "Growing Pains"; *Borderlands: Texas Poetry Review*: "Pilgrimage," "Sanctuary"; *Café Review*: "Empty Nest"; *Context South*: "Cremation" (published as "The Last Arms"); *di-verse-city*: "Undertow"; *di-verse-city 2000*: "Comfort Inn"; *El Locofoco*: "Christmas Sojourn"; *eNteLechY*: "Properties of Division"; *Entre Nous*: "Walls"; *Incongruous on Congress*: "Bell Peppers"; *Limestone Circle*: "Wilshire Woods"; *Main Street Rag*: "Family Values"; *Mañana*: "Daring," "Fall Garden, Texas," "Green Beans," "Potatoes," "Tomatoes," "Zucchini"; *modern words*: "Hunger," "Scrabble"; *No Shades of Gray*: "Continental Drift"; *Our Voice*: "Homophobia"; *Patchwork Poems*: "Onions," "Peas"; *Paterson Literary Review*: "Recovery"; *Poesia Y Calle*: "Birthday"; *Poetic Eloquence*: "Anniversary"; *Poetic Space*: "Sadomasochism"; *Poetry Motel*: "Reality"; *RE:AL*: "Nose Ring"; *RFD: A Country Journal*: "Close Enough"; *Shotgun Blast*: "Discretion"; *Southern Breezes* [PoetWorks Press, 2000]: "Confessional," "Cremation," "Humus," "Reality"; *Spillway*: "Mattress"; *très di-verse-city*: "Photograph"; *utter*: "Modern Labor," "Subtext"; *Voices Along the River*: "Room with a View"; *Will Work for Peace: New Political Poems* [Zeropanik Press, 1999]: "Scarecrow."

Contents

Corn   77

Green Beans   85

Eggplant   95

Potatoes   105

Tomatoes   117

Peas   125

This book is sincerely dedicated
to the many poets I've been inspired,
befriended, and encouraged by,
those from the
Austin Writers' League—
Jill, Christine, Mary-Agnes, Robin, Marcelle, Mikus—,
those from the
Austin International Poetry Festival—
Frank, Thom, Angela, Steve, Stazja, Pat, Peggy—
those from my online critique group,
Poetry-W—
Mary Alice, Claire, Karen, Quentin, Pam—
those from the
Cornerstone and Queer Poets series—
Cindy, Tommie, Joelle, Meera, Chinwe—
those I've had the great fortune to read,
hear, work, and publish with—
Susan, Ramona, Brett, Sonya, Renee, Garland—
those I've failed to mention
who write, read, and promote poetry,
and most of all
to the poet of my heart,
David.

Creation

A proud and expectant parent,
I thrill at this womb, my garden.

From conception
through gestation,
I feed, I nourish,
I orchestrate each natal step.
No change in weight
nor switch in position
escapes my watchful eye.
I am heavy with hope.

I treasure each meager thump
as seedlings kick through soil
in search of their first whit of breath.
I marvel anew at the miracle,
the lively folds of tiny green fingers.

I beam like I've delivered a world.

ASPARAGUS

Veritable Vegetable Company

Asparagus

I froze my ass off all winter,
doing my drag queen thing:
swayed in lacy little fronds,
primped in the frilliest finery,
swaggered in chichi fernery.
But don't think for a minute
that I don't like being a man;
like *The Crying Game*,
I've been hiding surprises.

Already a bold warmth
thrusts through my groins,
and I fill the bed with the
flair of a virulent violet,
a peck of green penes,
long and strong and erect,
a sea of charmed snakes
rising through the air, girl,
not once, but all spring long.

Discretion

The movie was foreign, forgettable.
I couldn't follow it anyway
for I was swept away by your presence,
attraction alluring as the moon's pull.
I would have touched you in the near-empty theater,
but even in the dark I feared their eyes,
so for two cruel hours I sat
on hands tingly with prickly impatience.

Later we parked outside my apartment.
I roped my tongue around yours,
sucked it like a hard candy
addictively flavored with coffee and tobacco.
Two stories up from the streetlight
my wife watched my appetite fog the windshield,
an engine purring with passion
blind as the wild tide.

Being Human

When I hold you,
it's not to make
a political statement.
When my hand rests
warmly in yours,
it's not to prove
a point to the world.
The world fades
far in the background,
fizzles to white noise
when I'm with you.
My kisses have
no hidden agenda.
I am just
a man in love
with another
human being,
who happens
to be a man.

Undertow

Two boxes of tampons
idle in the bathroom.
Her make-up cakes
in closed cabinets,
alongside phials
of expired pills.

An homage to Mrs. Onassis,
a case of champagne
huddles in the kitchen.
Her mother's cups
still clutter the counter.

With their broken spines,
her fantasies and mysteries
line the living room walls.
Her unwatched videotapes
brood under the TV.

Mail with her name
continues to gather
like dust on the desk
in the darkened study.

I sense empty blouses,
a potpourri of perfume,
buried deep in the closets.

Her dour family looks down
from photographs in the bedroom.
I lie on her side of the bed
hearing the ticking of clocks,
furnace's flare-ups,
occasional spasms of your sleep—
all the household sounds
to which she'd been accustomed.

I am an intruder, a voyeur.
This home will always be hers.

Hunger

You've seen the hollowed eyes,
peering through curtains of barbed wire
like black holes collapsing in space;
the throats, choking on human ash,
swallowing more death than life.

Stripped, shorn, and deloused,
starved to identical skeletal figures,
raw sticks of men transformed
from who to what by a swatch of cloth,
a hierarchy of colored triangles
where even murderers fared better
than men stitched pink with shame.

In a place as loveless as rock,
death was the law of averages,
yet desire, that tenacious weed,
wielded its way through concrete.

Men still felt its powerful pull,
mouths agape like fish on hooks,
hands as charged as electrified fences,
stony pupils staring down the distance
between flesh and fantasy.
The hope and the horror:
to touch without touching.

The purest expression
is the silence that resonates thunder.

Subtext

I'm not thinking about
the mouth of the man on stage,
whose lips pour out grief
over the loss of a lover
in lines sculpt from pain.

I'm not thinking about
the invitation burning
in the cosmic gaze
of the man in the second row
when his smoky eyes meet mine.

I'm not thinking about
the impeccably pink neck
of the student in the front row,
the one you used to nibble
shortly before you met me.

I'm thinking about you,
beside me in a row all our own,
wondering if what you saw
in this student half your age
is the same vulnerability
those molten eyes spot in me.

Size Queen

My first
was barely five inches,
fine for a first,
but quickly disappointing.

I thought
that I'd found heaven
when I had a taste of twelve,
yet even a foot proved
ultimately inadequate.

My mouth
began to water
when I sighted seventeen.
Now I've renounced
anything smaller.

Bigger *is* better
when it comes
to monitors.

B E E T S

Veritable Vegetable Company

Beets

You must pry their hold on the earth,
where dark magenta bulbs
with tails like dried-up tampons
are dense and dirty and deep.

You must chop off their tops,
while their stain rouges your fingers
and blushes down your arms,
flaring like a fiery fever.

You must boil them in a burgundy bath
and slip off their skins
like a pile of bludgeoned pelts,
slick and steamy and sweet.

You must slice and section,
feel your mouth gnaw and gnash,
scarlet as masticated glass:
nothing bleeds as endlessly as a beet.

Betrayal

This thing has grown
like a quiet anger,
boring its way in my body.

I would have expected pain,
a thread of blood,
at least a rash, an itch—
but I felt nothing.

This smudge of pigment
no different than sixty others
scattered about my skin.
The recent crater in my leg
attests to the mole's removal.
Now the biopsy proves it perverted.
More flesh must go:
this melanoma is malignant.

The immediacy of cancer
can't shake my disbelief.
This spot was no larger
than a pencil's width,
so unlike the abnormalities
on posters around the office:
this is not
how death should look.

I watch the doctor anesthetize
a circle the size
of a small coaster.
Wide and deep,
he scalpels through my skin.
I think of Shylock.
I still feel nothing.

But now the blood comes,
spreading out
like a thick vein of red rust.
I mop it with gauze,
for the office is closed,
and I must serve as nurse.
I'm not convinced of the urgency.

A final scrape
with a surgical tool
and the excision is complete.
I see two shaved flaps
of bleeding leg skin
sewn together
like a Nazi lampshade.

Only then do I realize
that I have been feeding death
like a ravenous houseguest;
that my body
has finally betrayed me.

Comfort Inn

They hide in corners like cobwebs,
lurking low in the carpet
like crumbs or slivers of glass.
They hang in the air,
drifting like dust mites
or spores from dirty filters.
The curious room rages
with strangers' nightmares.

A dog becomes an unfaithful wife.
A hawk rips off your roof.
The moon turns a furious purple
and stalks you to a lagoon.
You sink in its warm water
for you have no arms to swim:
your children have chewed them off.
The water is black and blood-red.

You wake with the residue
of dreams dark on your lips.
Something moves in the shadows,
in the carpet and corners,
as your dreams find a place
for the next unwary traveler.

Pruning (or The Modern Prometheus)

Occasionally it becomes necessary
to remove an unnecessary limb.
It might become bent or gnarled.
It might block desirable views.
It might cause excessive pain.

Lorena had no use for it,
so she hacked it off
like a mischievous branch
and tossed it in a field to compost.

A horde of horrified horticulturists
couldn't let detached things lie.
They grafted the limb back together.
Sure it was somewhat crooked,
angled like a partial erection,
stitched like the seams
of a soggy baseball.

But the graft proved interesting
to the world of inquiring minds.
John Wayne Bobbitt was recreated,
a miracle of macho science,
an Internet wonder, a cut-rate porn star.
All because Lorena had failed to practice
the proper techniques for pruning.

Fears of the Father

You hammered the words to my palate,
crushed my hand with a viper's grip
and spoke with an engineer's precision:
"At only one time in our lives
will you be exactly half my age."
I was twenty; you were forty.
Now I've reached forty, Dad.
I've forgiven but not forgotten.

Blinded, I groped in the basement,
stumbled over steps,
searching for scraps you'd throw my way.
I failed to find a key.
I choked on the dark,
cried through shell-shocked eyes,
thick with the soot of your love.

You were jailer and punisher,
the man of straps and restraints.
You were nightmare and maker,
the brute of battles and belts.

I was your prisoner of war.
Cowered in a corner,
I crushed my ears with my palms,
hearing only the surge of fear.

With your smoldering black shovel,
you hollowed out my heart,
mired and muddied it,
covered and tamped it tight.
Gasping and gutted,
slow as a archeological dig,
I scooped through the ruins
with the curse of the earth tones.
I excavated.

I was seeded with your demons,
your terrors were buried in my genes.
Sealed and sterile,
neutered as an empty jar,
slick as a pustule,
I scraped muck from my heart.

I picked through scabs
and bled through scars,
but I couldn't get through the black hole.
You could have left me
more than your void,
enormous, starless,
an implosion, an inkwell.
You should have left me more.

Sadomasochism

You never asked if it hurt.
I never asked you to stop.
Never ask questions:
the prime rule of our relationship.

Charge, retreat,
charge, retreat:
a springboard of desires,
a stiff reverberation in the bedroom.

You'd ride your tongue
across the ridge of my scar,
a six-inch stimulant,
like Warhol's, you said,
Andy without the wig.
Rule number two:
never be ourselves.

At times my blood
soaked through to the mattress,
coloring a battle map
of your brute campaigns,
a dark record of my decrement.

Sex was your sedative.
Many a thick midnight
I'd flee from your side
to curl like a handcuff
on the living room floor,
nursing pinched nipples
and crying like a mute.

Other times, two blocks away,
I'd stumble through parking lots
like an empty aluminum can.

Had the police stopped
to ask what I was doing,
I could honestly have said,
"I don't know."

I'd return to our bed
like an addict to a dealer—
you never knew I was gone.
If you did, you never let on.
Rule number three:
never say more than necessary.

Such was our relationship,
a crimped instrument of torture.
I thought I could find a little love;
all I discovered was more pain.

Close Enough

Somehow, even with our bodies
bound together like pages to a spine,
I can't be close enough to you.

I want to push my hands inside you.
I want to meld together
like halves of a factory mold.
I want to be a part of you,
as I want you to be part of me.

When you move your arm,
a tongue of muscle will race
down my backbone;
when you arch your foot,
a robust tug will dart to my groin.

Your lungs will be my lungs;
when you inhale, I will fill
with your rubied breath.
Your ventricles will be my lifeline,
shooting vitality to my extremities,
warm with vermilion passion.
Our hearts will tick
in synchronized rhythms,
a ballet of blood,
a union of cause and effect.

We could be fastened together
like teeth of a zipper.
Still I wouldn't be close enough.

ZUCCHINI

Veritable Vegetable Company

Zucchini

They grow in spurts,
these wild zucchini,
adolescents out of control.

Itching for thrills,
they strut down streets
like landlords:
they've taken over the hood.

They roam cocksure through yards,
they creep boldly over fences,
they read "keep out" signs as "come in."

They tag their territory
with verdant graffiti.
They spray "ZOOKS"
on bus stops and walls.

They wear tough like armor.
They're James Dean in green.
They think they'll live forever.

But a knife hovers over
these brash young zucchini,
to cut them in their prime.

Walls

The son sullies like a pharaoh
sealed in his dead room,
hair dyed as black as rage
or a cauldron of raucous rock.

Fists balled into hammers,
the father spits like a runaway wire,
pounds and pounds on lifeless pine,
framing frustration with each futile blow.

They have fashioned a language
of carpenter's lines and gestures,
a physical language that buttresses walls,
walls constructed without ears.

Hardhats firmly in place,
toolbelts anchored in position,
they are architects of attitude,
sweaty with misspent anguish and pain.

Piers and beams support the silence;
spaces muffle meanings and feelings.
The father can no more hear his son
than the son can hear his father.

Building barren new walls is easier
than tearing the old ones down.
For some fathers and sons,
it's the only thing done well together.

Dumbing Down

Arrogant in their ignorance,
they stare at stacks
with the glaze of the unfamiliar.
Bookcases are some weird wallpaper,
crammed with patterns
of dead men's opinions.
The library is a morgue,
unread books like bodybags
piled on shelves
beyond the reach
of these unread students.

Reading is irrelevant;
print is passé.
As long as their walls become lined
with degrees and diplomas,
they have all the words they need.
Their pockets might be stuffed
with keys to Mercedes and plastic—
always plenty of plastic—
but their eyes will remain
as vacant as paper.
These are the proud,
these are the many,
these are the graduates
of the new education.

Booting Up

With worlds at their fingertips,
they stare at flamboyant monitors
splattered with dungeons and violence,
ever faster, ever more lifelike.
They maneuver through mazes
with the skill of a surgeon.
They never learned to spell
"maneuver" or "surgeon."

Life's trapdoors are another problem,
far trickier than monsters and land mines.
Cloaked in log-ins of anonymity,
they take refuge in private rooms,
where they lie to strangers
with four-letter words
and a handful of one-word responses.

Bleached by high resolution,
spellbound by screens
of insipid video clips,
they feed on the fodder of microchips.
No bang, no whimper,
their world will end with a blip.

Proctor

The classrooms are no different
from the ones in my high school:
paint the color of dirty fish tanks,
blinds that never quite close,
fluorescent lights that flicker erratically,
posters that warn of drugs' dangers,
fading with crackled Scotch tape.

These students clutch number two pencils
with fingers close to the lead,
filling bubble after bubble in black
to prove that they can read.

I'm the only Anglo here.
My list shows names like Vargas,
Vasquez, Ramos, Ybarra.
Black-haired, brown-eyed,
all have taken this test before.
None will graduate without it.

One is uncomfortably pregnant;
another, fast asleep.
One stares wildly at the wall
as if having a religious vision.
Another peels splinters
from a graffitied desktop.
One traces the tattooed letters
webbed between his fingers.
Some seem to be trying.

The next proctor finally arrives.
We don't need to worry about cheating.
We succeeded at that long ago.

Daring

We would play a game
in college called "Accident."
Speeding down a highway,
having smoked more reefer
than government guinea pigs,
we'd cover the eyes of the driver
with our wet mittens and gloves,
screeching like banshees,
"Accident! Accident!"
and laughing as if this were
the funniest thing in the world.

We age, we shrink.
Our definition of daring narrows:
an afternoon walk in the woods,
no sticks, no mace,
no sleeves on our shirts,
no sunscreen.

Defense Mechanisms

Roland
The thing I remember about Roland
is the bookbag straddled across his chest,
clutched as if it were a baby.
You'd think he was protecting Fort Knox,
not just books or school supplies.
I never saw Roland without the bag,
even during P.E., when I'd see him running laps
outside my library windows, alone.

Champagne
The thing I remember about Champagne,
the black girl who was anything but bubbly,
is that white people were always "racial."
I told her she meant "racist,"
but this just proved that I was "racial."
I stumped her the day I told her my girlfriend was black,
moreso because she knew I was married.
Champagne had blue eyes.

Nguyen
The thing I remember about Nguyen is that,
other than an occasional hello,
I never heard her speak English.
Her twin sister Nga prattled in English and Korean.
Both sisters had been in the U.S. for two years,
but Nga was as Americanized
as Nguyen remained Old World.
When Nga was around, Nguyen faded like furniture,
but smiled.

Continued

Helen
The thing I remember about Helen
is the vicious mouth, thin and curled,
surrounded by a shapeless clump of crow-black hair.
Teachers were natural targets, but Helen
reserved her worst sarcasm for her classmates.
She was not afraid to back up her mouth with her fists,
with a strength that belied her size.
She is the only junior high student I've ever known
to read the *New York Times*,
which she brought to school each day
so she'd have something to do.

Jose
The thing I remember about Jose
is the day he called me a bitch.
By the time Jose's parents were summoned to school,
"bitch" had become "bifocals."
His mother never said a word during the conference,
his father believed him, the principal agreed.
I must have been mistaken.
The next day when Jose smirked at me
from behind his five-foot macho facade,
I called him something
that could have been construed as "bifocals."

Stanley
The thing I remember about Stanley
is the winter camouflage jacket he'd wear
through every season of the year.
Stanley had cats, and every one of them
must have marked that jacket.
You could smell Stanley coming
before you ever saw him,
yet he always seemed amazed

that I could detect his presence.
Stanley's brother Clifford also wore a camouflage jacket,
the same dingy color of old tents,
the same rank smell that kept others at bay.

Vicky
The thing I remember about Vicky
is how boys were attracted to her
like alcoholics to booze.
She was not particularly pretty,
but neither diseases nor abortions
diminished her appeal.
She finally left school six months pregnant
by Lee, her pregnant sister's older boyfriend.
Lee wore a leather jacket with chains.
He still owes me a book.

Accomplice

Aiding and abetting
is how I spend my days
at the high school library.

They come to me—
not for a good book—
but for the shortest one, the easiest one,
the one they read in junior high
or that's been made into a movie.

I've tried to guide them
toward *good* books,
but my powers of persuasion
have gone the way of catalog cards.

I tell myself that
at least they're reading something,
and something is better than nothing.
But when books are renewed
and bookmarks remain lodged
like poppy seeds between teeth
just pages into the first chapter,
I know this too is a lie.

I seldom order anything over 200 pages,
anything reviews call "challenging" or "literary."
I censor by not purchasing
books of style or substance.
Most of my budget goes to trash—
books on drugs, witches, tattoos,
books with more pictures than pages,
books where sex and violence rule.

I feel guilt for my part in this crime.
The only crime they recognize
is having been made to read.

O N I O N S

Veritable Vegetable Company

Onions

We're not as transparent
as you might expect.

We just hide our hurt well,
behind layers and layers
of skin as thin as film,
wound tight as plastic wrap.

We bury our fears
in concentric tiers:
repression is our forte.

We shade our afflictions
in multi-plied wisps.
From sheer sheets of paper
we make masks
to conceal our cache of pain.

Like stone in a cavern,
we weep deep inside.
Slice through to our core,
and you too will suffer our tears.

Recovery

I settle back into myself
like dust slowly filters
through an open screen window.

The rush of love has worn off.
Reason has returned.
The show is over.
What you call change,
I call recovery.

Gauze had clouded my eyes,
but I've been unwinding it layer by layer.
I now see past your fancy veneer,
your decorative antique molding.
They're not attached to anything.
Were you always so ephemeral?

When I gaze into my mirror,
I'm surprised to like what I see:
no visible scars, no hint of a head-on,
no tortured emotions blocking my way.

If you could see me now
as clearly as I see you,
you'd know that I am in control,
that love starts and stops with me.

Continental Drift

When did you become
a foreign country?

When did I start
needing translation?

When did your borders
barricade themselves?

How did my exchange rate
lose its currency?

How did our latitudes
become distant lines?

How does love shrink
to a geography lesson?

Principles of Perspective

Our days have reached a horizon.

Already your cloudy blues
retire like sight to the sky,
while warm colors of solitude
advance in space around me.

I rode fate like a comet
to see where it would lead.
Drawn to your black hole,
I journeyed past
the vanishing point,
flung to the fringe
of the unfamiliar.

I burned with your intensity,
imploded in your darkness.

I have found my way back
to a one-point perspective,
to quiet rules that I don't question:
lines that converge in one direction,
planes that merge into points,
details that fade to gray—

one day at a time,
the way we said we'd take it.

Properties of Division

History is divisible by two.

The proof is in her albums,
littered with spaces where I once existed,
holes from which I've been exhumed.

The proof is in a recycled sack,
a mishmash of snapshots that I've been apportioned,
a medley of allotted memories.

The proof is in our separate shares of eighteen years,
the fervent photos of friends and follies,
the families, feasts, and happy hours.

(Cameras never capture the woe.)

The paradox of this mad mathematics
is the odd quotient of the equation:
half of eighteen can still be the whole.

History is divisible by two,
but somehow there's always a remainder.

Anniversary

So you've left for Mesa Verde
with our old cooler, our old tent,
and your newfangled lover.
You've got bug-spray and band-aids,
phone numbers and film.
You've got everything, baby,
but me.

It's the first anniversary
of the night you left me
with faith in myself abandoned.
We staked out the constructs
of our relationship long ago:
I was always the sinner,
you were always the saint.
You were my social worker and savior,
good cop to my bad one.

I'm such a slow unlearner:
I've only now begun
to peel away the programming
of so many married years
and break the choke-chain
of our self-induced boundaries.
I've only now begun to realize
that you can play the sinner,
that I can play the saint,
that we choose our own roles,
that we write our own scripts.

So wander carefree in Colorado,
sleep soundly with powdery ghosts.
I'll dream of our distance alone.

Nose Ring

I am not staring at you
because of the ring in your nose,
though I assume that *is* the point.
I am staring because
it looks like *my* ring
swinging between your nostrils,
and I am wondering
how you managed to
get it through the cartilage,
not to mention
out of my closet,
where I laid it to rest
when my marriage
got all gristly.
I am staring because
I want to see how you eat
with the smell of failure
dangling under your nose.

Striptease

Before I started the slow unraveling,
I was layered like a mummy,
wrapped in fear so stifling,
I was hesitant to breathe.

Haltingly—a fingertip, a toe—
a turtle emerging from its shell,
apprehensive to experience a world
I dared not dream could be.

More fear unwound, more flesh bared—
a patch of arm, a clearing of calf—
reticence flaking from my frame
like years of weathered paint.

Fibers and fabric fell to the floor—
a chest revealed, a thigh uncovered—
and lightness replacing those leaden fears
I'd been enveloped in for years.

In the awkward dance of knowing,
I've cast off many veils.
I will strip and get more bold,
till I can bear my body naked.

BELL PEPPERS

Veritable Vegetable Company

Bell Peppers

One by one
these cages have emptied,
my brothers taken away.
I'm the last one left
on this row of death.
All appeals have expired.

My walls are thick,
my membranes, strong.
My stem's grown tough
as I've served my time.
Yet tonight I'm sentenced
to lose what's left
of what little is still mine.

Awake and alone
I gaze from my gloom,
murmuring laments
like a bell that has
lost its tongue.
My prayers are mute.
My God is gone.

I am not ready.
I am not guilty.
I have never been so hollow.

Christmas Sojourn

(for Brad Wiggerman)

You are leaving home for Christmas,
past fields paralyzed with frozen stalks
that make you think of bones.
Although the heat is on high,
you are cold to the tips of your fingers,
where you clutch yet another cigarette,
inhaling for evidence of life.

You are far from the home
where you took yourself hostage—
lights out, shades down, sealed off
for days in your own private hell.
Arms flailing and mind amuck,
you were consumed by the burn,
a prisoner of endless white lines,
your sole ambition
to sleep and never awake.

You are on an icy highway
to a place of no calls, no visits,
to a house that's halfway
to who knows what.
They are waiting for you
to remove the one thing
that has given you comfort—
no joy—all these years.
They are waiting for you
to smother the cocaine
that crowds out your reason,
to raze the drifts in your head.
They are waiting
to bring you back.

You are far from home
but too near to pain.
The barren furrows shiver
beyond the car windows,
as you watch the colored lights
of a lonely farmhouse
blinking in the silent distance.

Confessional

(for Mary Dicks)

I hold your lust to my ear,
hear your promiscuous thoughts
as you cross your legs,
squirm like a penitent,
cover your mouth quickly,
afraid God will read your lips.
You choke on mild profanity,
blush with a ruttish flush.
Mary, if you knew that I sit here nude,
your heated sweat of holy water
would dribble through this phone.

On the morning of our first communion
you clipped a crucifix around your neck;
it hangs there still, only tighter, like a noose.
You shun the looks of reproachful priests
lest they recognize the spent desires
spilled out in your last confession.
You cower to your knees on Sundays
and swallow the body and blood of Christ,
already repentant in the connotations
of this sexiest of sacraments.

"I'm sorry" trails from your lips
like the shiny beads of a rosary.
The daily flail, the coarse hair shirt,
you thrash your back at every chance
for imaginary transgressions.
You have made an art of apology.
You are the perfect supplicant.

God has siphoned all your faith
and hollowed out your self-esteem.
You fawn through life's stark stations,
wallowing in religious wreckage.
I've crawled free, but lost my soul.
Hail, Mary, pray for me.

Pilgrimage

A morning sun tints green pines red.
It is crisp in the Sangre de Cristos.
A powerful balm of piñon,
a flutter of mountain aspen—
almost enough to forget vacant villages,
quiet pueblos of faded clay
baked till they all look the same.

The room is filled with words
neglected in English dictionaries.
Latillas, *vigas*—somehow more exotic
than cheap cedar poles and unfinished beams.
Rough-hewn chairs of *equipale*,
a glowing kiva that brings
kachinas' shadows to life.
Outside, under the *portales*,
are the requisite antlers and skulls
that tourists have come to expect.

The square is lined with silver and turquoise,
a place where marketing meets land:
bright-colored weavings, dyed corn necklaces,
Ácoma pottery, *ristras* of dried red chiles.
Corners are crowded with sunburnt hawkers
of Navajo tacos and Indian fry-bread.
But I will dine in a pricey *placita* where
blue corn tortillas are topped with fried eggs
and customers are whiter than linen.

The city is a church,
santos in every niche,
enough tin crosses
for dozens of stations.
Farolitos flicker down streets
like a glimpse of peace,
a taste of heaven.
I walk on a dusting of snow,
filled with a faith
that the place is holy,
as only some places can be.
My heart climbs a ladder
that leads to a blue sky
for it finds no doors down below.

The Heart of January

The fitful crackle of the fireplace,
sleet like static on the windowpane,
and I languish between
the rhythms of fire and ice,
the incessant echoes of despair.

I wait like an ice fisherman
with a pole but no pick
at a hole that's freezing over,
a life on interminable hold.
I wait like a man with a prayer.

Maybe this is what a new year's about:
struggling to stay warm by a hearth
when the heart has gone stone cold,
trying to wait out resolutions
when we need to kindle dreams.

Coming and Going

You left again last night,
shifted like a ghostly cloud
to somewhere I'm not allowed.

That place must be special
for you seem to be smitten
with sudden visits all too often.

You don't hear voices—
not the ones I hear—
and your empty eyes, I fear,

see nothing mine do,
staring like those of a mannequin.
I can pinch your pale skin

or squeeze your scrawny knee,
but I can't break the cadence
of this strong indulgence.

I've run out of tricks
doing cartwheels for you.
Drift back, daddy, indulge in me too.

Lost and Found

Stuffed in the corner of a closet
on a shelf too high to reach,
a crusty box with tape so withered
it peels like bark beneath your nails.

You no longer remember
having buried that box,
though its contents are vaguely familiar:
scraps of newspapers,
lifeless photographs,
letters as brittle as bone—
things as sealed from life as corpses.

From a yellowed envelope
you extract a letter penned in red,
its words full of dim love.
You used to read them late at night
and dream of the morning.
You no longer dream.
You don't even recognize
the handwriting.

Pasted to the back
of a picture is a poem
that reads like a bad translation,
though once it made you cry.
You spot aimless words
like *Love* and *Forever,*
words that are only words.

Corners of faded photographs
crumble at your touch.
You recall no names for most of the faces;
those you do are nothing but names.
Colors have dissolved like memory.

There's no preserving this life,
so you discard the box reluctantly.
Time is running out,
and you've still so many
other things to pack.

Room with a View

No matter how hard I try,
I see only three walls in this room—
      three deafening wooden walls
      where man has left his musk,
      time has left its stains,
      patience, its tinge—
and a silent white ceiling.

Triangles have only three walls,
but I see only two corners,
      and I know that triangles
      have three straight walls,
      three creased corners,
      and an ample amount of space.
This triangle's too delicate to face.

The ceiling plays with the light from a window,
light that avoids the walls as well as me.
      Triangles shift across the ceiling,
      waves and waves,
      leaving streams of life
      in the shadows —
till they disappear amidst the brittle quiet.

I'd like to see the fourth wall
without the sorrow of two more corners,
      but the fourth wall,
      the vacant wall,
      like so much else,
      is behind me.

ARTICHOKE

Veritable Vegetable Company

Artichoke

An artichoke is
the chart to this heart.

This heart is dangerous,
a thumping, thistly
fist of a thing,
a pumping, prickly
knot of green.

This heart is hidden,
its pulp protected
by spiny locks,
its pith secured
in a safety box.

This heart is demanding,
a convoluted, arduous
trail to venture,
a deep, delicious
delicacy to savor.

The art to this heart
is an artichoke.

A Perfect Fit

To wake in your spoon
is to know my place in the world,
a place not large but right.

Closely nestled like coves of petals,
secure against evening's frost,
I shut my eyes in darkness

and count time with your breath
whispering against my neck,
a sound as rhythmic as rocking.

You can more than balance the world.
Content to settle into your spoon,
I need nothing else today, tonight.

Of Distance and Lovers

You're two thousand miles away.
I measured the distance in an atlas,
traced the tepid greens and blues
around cold coves of Puget Sound.
I found the island you called from;
what I wanted to find was you.

While you were watching the ferry's wake,
I took your cologne from my counter,
rubbed it in slowly, the way you always do.
Then I took your scent to bed like a lover,
where I felt your breath nestle at my neck,
your gentle fingers twine into mine.
We lulled to sleep in identical climes.

I awake sticky from last night's dreams.
The morning here is Houston humid.
Heat hisses off the blacktop
like steam from fresh-brewed coffee.
Morning makes it easy to believe
that miles are merely a mirage.

Compromise

The last of you
runs down the drain
with suds as ghostly
as last night's moon.
Like a kidney donor,
I am reluctant but willing,
having given up a part of me
to have a part of you.
Love is the compromise
that allows the self to sacrifice.

Endless bills pile up
like stacks of dirty dishes;
letters lie unanswered
and magazines are unread.
Everyday chores
gather like household dust.
My words float unattached
to any piece of paper.
Under your strong spell,
hours flee like phantoms.
Time now manages me.

I step out of the shower,
breathing deep your residue,
holding close the space
that was a part of me
that's now a part of you,
glad to have exchanged so little
to have gotten back so much.

Mattress

Our crooked bodies curl like cats
in a knot in the center of the bed.
I like that beneath us is a mattress
on which no one but us has slept,

a strong, hard mattress,
made for middle-aged backs,
for stomachs unreined in the night,
for necks that slope into folds.

Deep creases clothe your nape,
shadows that coil into the pillow.
Neck hairs bristle in scraps of moonlight,
glimpses of glistening silver.

Your heavy breath fills the room.
I listen till my own lungs
match your respiration,
and I lull toward repose.

Second Season

Not as forgiving as chalky sycamores
beseeching bare-armed the sky,

nor as wise as the tonsured peaks
of mountains ghostly with snow.

Not as tenacious as raw-throated rocks
bleached stark-white in the desert,

nor as courageous as salty waves
cresting the deep-sinewed waters.

Not as tranquil as fallow fields
frosted by winds' hoary breath,

nor as experienced as raging rivers,
alight with silver-rimmed winter.

Yet you are here with me,
grand as anything seasoned by Nature.

I ask for nothing more than to celebrate
the next fifty years together.

Wilshire Woods

Dragonfly summer comes to an end;
temperatures at last are tolerable.
Pecans tumble onto the roof,
intermittent as the ping
of beetles at the screen.
Too dazed with autumn to scamper,
front porch geckos hug the bricks.
Sycamore leaves in windswept swirls
settle in heaps by the fence.
There's nowhere else to go.

We will walk tonight
in the full moon's sheen
past alleys and post oaks,
down dark city streets
skittish with faded foliage.
The scene is familiar.
Your hand brushes mine,
your eyes dance colors.
We revel in a cool simmer
like insects off in the distance.

Fall Garden, Texas

Overhead the trees shed watercolors,
blurs of browns and yellows
like so many discarded washes.

Below, fingernails of onion
claw seekingly from the ground;
lazy zucchini stretch out,
hang impishly over their bed;
spinach bunches in muscles
like tight little drums.
The herbs still think that it's spring.

From a window I watch
the cool of this season
feed my crazy green salad
with a litter of leaves,
glad that I planted myself
in your warm kitchen.

C O R N

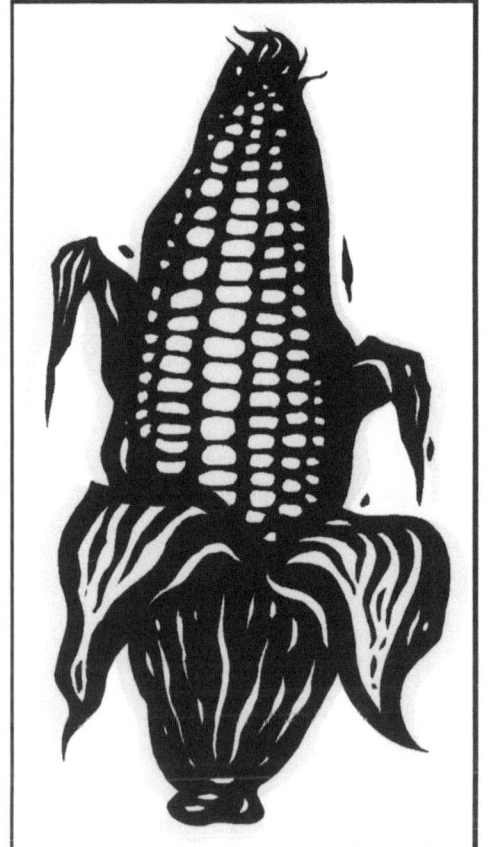

Veritable Vegetable Company

Corn

Off come the husks,
shucked in a quick striptease.
Off come the strands of silk,
carefully, like fine French underthings.
Shorn of these threads,
into a hot tub they're plunged.

Out they come, dripping wet,
circled by swirls of steam.
Slathered and bathed in butter,
bright as neon yield signs,
sweet kernels spew forth
their sticky milk sugars,
drain juice down chins like drool.
Ears are nibbled to nubs,
cobs are sucked to the marrow.
The kitchen is filled with comestible moans.

You and I find ravishment
fresh from our Midwest fields.
Corn must be an Illinois thing,
for your husband
clearly misconstrues
our just-got-laid smiles.

Birthday

You just called
to say happy birthday
and to remind me
that you're not
speaking to me.

Still desire
prickles up my stomach
for no one
doesn't speak to me
like you do.

Beach Boy Summer

The phonograph surfed
an endless groove of
lift, creak, pause, and play,
filling your bedroom
with "Good Vibrations."

As long as I was Laura,
girl of your adolescent dreams,
it was okay to spread
your hands between my thighs
and gingerly peck my neck.
Our lips might graze
like long blades of grass,
before remembering the limits
of same-sex static.

If I called you Diane, the girl
you thought I'd want you to be,
it was okay to slide my hand
down your hairless stomach,
tickle and tackle your
fresh-sprung growth,
lose myself in our excitations.

By the time the Beach Boys
had become another nostalgia act,
you were stuck in automatic replay:
married the real Laura, divorced her,
and repeated the pattern
with your next three wives.

Now we can't even find 45s
or buy a turntable to play them.
But I'm thinking you're like me:
still picking up the reverberations
of our good, good, good vibrations.

Rowing

I coiled around you
like a sea serpent,
clutching your chest
all sleepless night,
squeezing out life
drop by intimate drop.
You abandoned my bed,
my morning yet scented
with your sweet brew.
Your taste lingers
like a holy hangover.
Your touch tingles
like a sudden tide.
Your long groans idle
in my ear's alcoves.
You left me lost at sea,
spent and reeling,
but rowing hard
to your snug shore.

Breakfast

We go to bed
like toast and butter.

I, the toast,
hot and stiff,
ready to be spread.

You, the butter,
cold and pliant,
eager to be melted.

All we need now is jam.

Into the Great Wide Open

sliding, gliding
our tongues tangoed
        dashed and dipped
    clasped and grasped
painting the small town pink

skimming, rimming
our tongues stepped out
        clicked and licked
    grazed and lazed
cutting loose on crazy palettes
    frisking on moist rooftops

boring, soaring
our tongues marathoned
        wider, honey, wilder
    groped and roped
till we tasted
    the lust of skylarks

GREEN BEANS

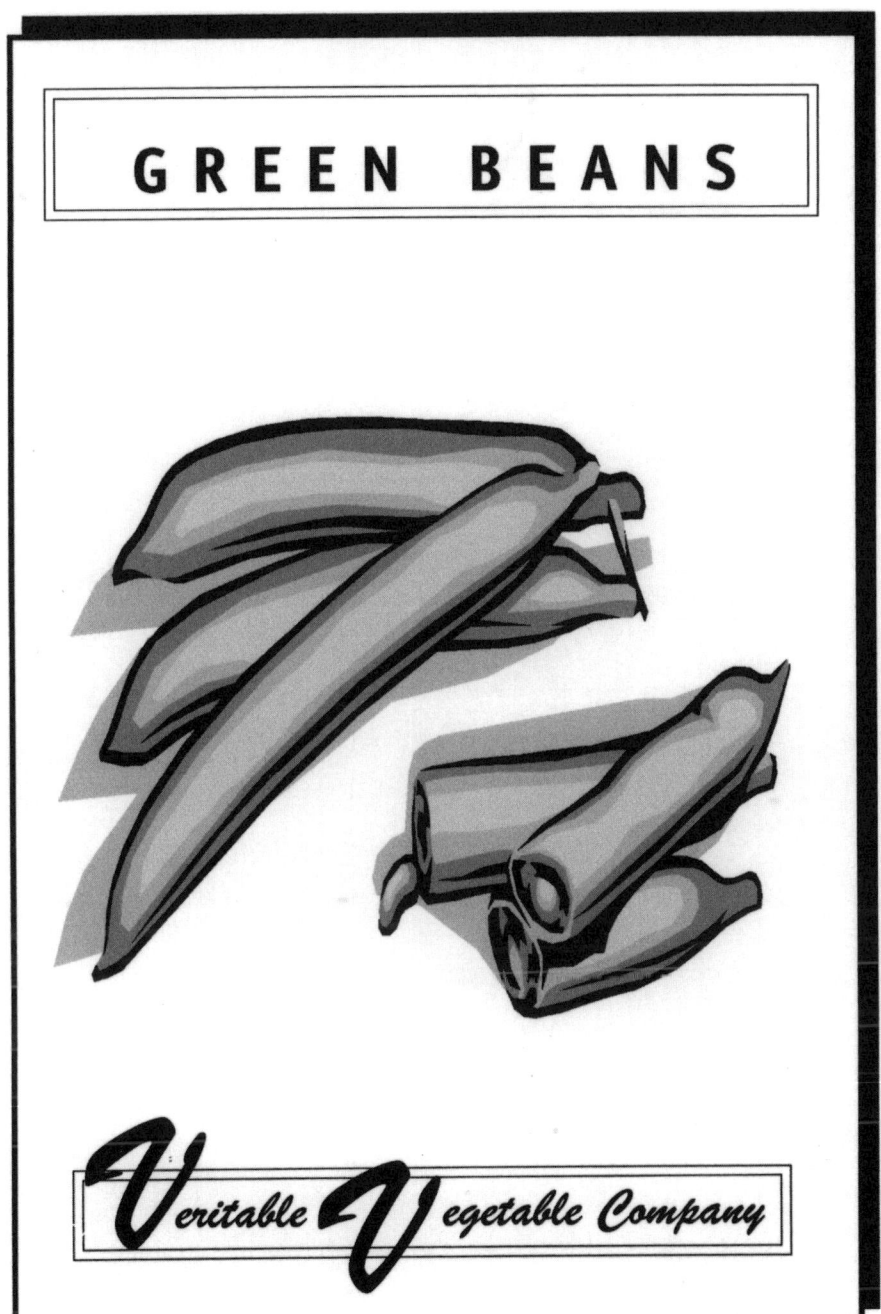

Veritable Vegetable Company

Green Beans

The beans are fertile
in this ghetto of crowded green.
The men spill seed like clockwork;
the women are factories of birth.
There are too many children
and no room to breathe;
packed in shacks like peanuts,
the youngest barely hang on.
They gasp, they hunger,
they fight each other for light.
There's never enough space,
there's never enough food,
but there will never be family planning
in this Third World of congested vegetables.
In a plot of natural selection,
they cry, they pray for survival.

Scarecrow

(for Matthew Shepard, 1976-1998)

To pull the trigger would have been too kind.
They broke your nose, crushed your brain stem,
battered your flesh till it grafted to bone;
left you burned, lashed to Laramie split-pine,
spread-eagled, barefoot, a bloodied gay totem.
The night froze black around a scarecrow alone.

A day later your body was discovered,
limp as the straw of a weathered bale.
You never came out of the coma; I pray
you slipped into it early in the night, hovered
at heaven's thin edge, unburdened and pale,
before hate spilled over to the light of day.

Closing Time

Labels peel in small white strips,
like birch bark under fingertips.

The patrons, too, are peeling,
like frayed tape on vinyl barstools
or wrinkled wallpaper, hazy with smoke.
Dull strips of deadened skin,
yellowed as yesterday's newsprint,
gather soundlessly at their feet.
Another bottle, damp as night sweats,
is all they've come to expect.

Life peels away in a slow eclipse,
draining like blood between long hard sips.

Modern Labor

They're lining up at Labor World,
cold breath and cigarette smoke
dissipating like dreams unfurled.
A block away even poorer folks
push grocery carts like Sisyphus
and scribble signs on scraps of wood
as they choke on soot from a city bus:
"God bless. Will work for food."
These are not Depression-era lines
of men who had something and lost it;
these are people born like vines
to walls of brick, no polish, no spit.
They sleep beneath the freeway's wail
in rags of dreams, doomed to fail.

Skeletons

Consider the closet:

deep recesses
of dead desires,
hollowed like a scarab

hooks hung loosely
with ectomorphic fashions,
remains of lapsed generations
left for relatives
to one day discover

shelves of shoe boxes,
repositories of memories,
letters and trinkets
layered like shoddy brickwork,
laid to silence
in a musty mausoleum

Somewhere in here
are graveyards of dreams
forgotten lives
shed like epidermis
in dark corners

where bones of the past
transform truth to mystery
where mystery turns to myth

Discontinued Patterns

As if one day could dispel
all the years that brought us here.
As if I could
close my eyes and call your name,
having forgotten the
fragile fragments we've become,
the travesties
of shattered evenings.
As if love would be enough
to glue the self together,
and then the separate selves.
As if all that matters
is something—anything—
that keeps the heart moving
or makes the mind whirl,
a song the same as separation.
At least we've tried
to hold the pieces together;
in fact, we've succeeded.
Only we no longer
recognize the pattern.

Grave Shift

Her leaden neck crooks
like a bent willow reed,
sagging so low
you expect to hear it snap.
Her backbone taut
with knobby protrusions,
as though a stone has skipped
the silent waters of her spine,
leaving small nodes in its wake.
Her skin seems to sallow
before your eyes,
leached to a nicotine yellow.
She plods closer to the counter,
her breath as forced
as her flagging shuffle.
You pass on the refill,
afraid the next cup
may be the one that
sends her back to the grave.

Growing Pains

An insignificant bead
filters from the ceiling
on an invisible string
of nothing.

We watch, miserably,
from the corners of the room
as a scant spider
accumulates importance.

EGGPLANT

Veritable Vegetable Company

Eggplant

I am dark.
I am different.
Handicapped by
an accident of genes,
a chance of chromosomes,
things I cannot control
any more than you.

My skin is purple
as a lesion,
murky as a black eye,
just thick enough
to insulate
a heart too often
creamy with tears,
beating like yours
beneath my veneer.

My head is as huge
as a hydrocephalic's.
I move slowly
because of my shape.
You call me special
and think you're polite,
but I have heard the names
you fail to whisper—
I am large;
I am not dumb.

Continued

Held hostage
by a body
I did not choose,
even at night
I don't dream
that I'm you.
I do wish
that you
could be me.

Homophobia

Blue is the color
of the dance of lonely men,
their longing and loathing
etched like sad calligraphy
in bags beneath their eyes.

The soles of their feet are bottomless,
as hard as the unpried shells
that mire them in desire and denial,
as painful as the hate harbored
in cold blue pockets inward.

They yearn to love another,
but till they learn to love themselves,
they'll dance alone a desperate dance
in the harrowing silence
of a pale midnight blue.

Bipolar

You wrap the wire round your head
so tight your eyes detect no light,
a muffled mouth, your words unsaid.

You hold your skull like *The Scream*,
a ball of silent barbs and spite,
a cavern blank, a dearth extreme.

I sense you've found a strange asylum,
a prison, too, all drab and white,
filled with fear and days of doldrum.

One becomes inured to coping,
so self-abuse can seem all right,
whatever it takes to keep on hoping—

radiation, toxicants, dialysis,
or your metallic lair to ease the bite
of a manic sweat or catatonic crisis.

I know you cry, I know you hurt.
I see the rust stains of your fright
that seep down toward a world of dirt.
I've been there too, I'm here tonight.

Sanctuary

Then she was the wallpaper,
reflected in criss-crossed patterns
of copper pots and silver spoons.

Tucked away like a linen napkin
in a drawer of cotton towels,
she no longer heard that voice,
shrill as a teapot whistle,
no longer smelled the trail
of scorched vegetables and Sanka.

She could survey from the wall,
review the room as if from a turret:
the nervous assortment of knives
with edges glistening like cut glass;
a lone canister, severely chipped,
with "flour" bleached into "our";
crumbs of love, kitchen offerings.

Then her heart hadn't crumpled,
dried like a heel of old white bread
petrified on a cold counter
cluttered with beer bottles and butts.

Wallpaper: where hands can't hurt
and desolate eyes can't surprise.
Just rich squares of repetition,
pots and spoons, spoons and pots.

The Gift Book

Already pages fade,
sharp edges go . . .

Inside you wrote no words,
yet your ruminations
appear in the print
like cryptics:
I read you oh so well.
I see the things you never told me,
things I never acknowledged,
things you and I both knew.

Then there's the photographs:
erotic, artistic,
the way you always wanted it—
and me.

I failed you,
or perhaps you failed me,
or maybe it doesn't matter anymore,
for my memory yellows
like the sperm-colored cover.

And though ghosts like this
are meant to be shelved,
this one lingers on:
tall, thin, pale,
persistent—
improperly placed away.

Chaos Theory

The sky is slate gray,
the oaks are empty,
and for a moment I think
I might still love you.
I laugh out loud to the wind,
knowing better than anyone
how absurd this notion sounds,
but emotions are not as predictable
as the loss of autumn's leaves
or the frost of winter's cold.

Love is a muddle of emotions,
the dada of the heart.
I have focused too long
on what's proved to be wrong.
To think that I love you
or that you could still love me
is as circular as the seasons,
as sensible as creation—
but even chaos has a theory.

Reality

Perhaps it is the history of green mornings
that calls us back to this place.
Though we don't see them,
our reflections are here somewhere,
flitting from shadow to shadow,
bouncing off clouded coffee cups
like moths in crowded rooms.
There are things best left unspoken.

It doesn't matter
if you don't remember the day.
Leftover days have been forgotten
or etched away anyway;
all that remains is what should remain.

When we leave this place,
as we gather the pieces of here and there,
I will think of you,
of the long dark afternoon,
of the sky smoldering so far in the distance,
so very far away.

POTATOES

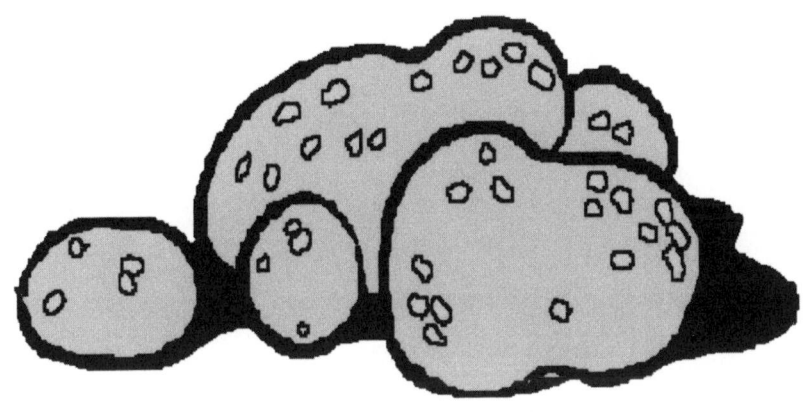

Potatoes

Our parents were potatoes,
severed and slaughtered,
buried in the shallowest of graves.

Left with nothing but vengeance
in veins vacant of being,
we were born in black earth,
our eyes crusted with dirt,
silent and shorn of a soul.

Now we've dug our way out,
drudging through daylight
in search of the living,
our pace stiff and slow,
mechanical as rigor mortis.

We're single-minded and hungry,
potatoes with a purpose,
and nothing will stop us but salt.

Family Values

My mother's lover
looked like a gorilla:
furry flat face, ridged brow,
flaring nostrils as wide as his eyes.
Thick was the thatch
of black bristles on his torso;
shirts couldn't hide
the shock of monkey suit beneath.

Like Samson, his hair brought him strength.
He would slaughter a steer
with his own immense hands
and deliver my mother some meat.
The freezer was kept in the basement;
the payment was made in the bedroom.
The door, like a cage, would latch shut,
and strains of muffled jungle rhythms
would reverberate out through the ducts.
Then to his truck he'd lurch
like a primate just set free.
She'd wave like Jane,
wearing little more than a loincloth.

I never snitched on my mother.
I seldom talked to my father,
though I'm certain the affair was no secret,
quite unlike my own private payback
with the son of gorilla,
the first boy to handle
my slippery banana.
Thanks, junior.

Fairy Tale

I'm washing streaky windows
and folding crumpled laundry,
filling the weekend hours
with our socks and underwear,
with dishrags and ashes.
You're off to your daddy's wedding,
a second wife, a second life,
leaving me with blues and a broom.

I'd have made a mockery of love,
a show of sin in living color.
So I was banished from Daddy's ball,
and you followed his proclamation.
Never mind that we found in each other
our own second lives and loves.
Never mind that my gay foot
perfectly fits your gay slipper.

Now you're dressed up and dancing,
enjoying a meal fit for a prince,
while I'm hours away, invisible,
scrubbing toilets on hands and knees,
living with inherited hypocrisy.

Icarus

Falling seaward with eyes to the sky,
I see your head in the clouds.
I want to see something
other than indifference—
a wince of regret, a tear.

As I plummet on errant wings,
as I crumple like a ball of paper,
ever the scientist, you watch,
calculate the force
of my impending impact,
predict the spot
my body will wash ashore.
Your mind moves
to the machine of myth;
mine has always looked
down to earth.

You were always too clever,
so bent on your own genius
that I could never be more
than a footnote for you.
The labyrinth you built for Minos
cannot compare to the one
you created for me.

I heard your warnings
about wax and feathers,
but I chose not to heed them.
Just once I wanted
to rise above your shadow,
to see the sun with no reproach,
free, Father, and fading.

Housecleaning

For you I scrubbed
the kitchen floors
and polished the
fireplace brass.
For you I vacuumed
vertical blinds,
ridding their cloth
of dander and dust.
My hands were scoured
by the chemicals of cleaning,
but my house was ready
for a white-glove test—
anyone's, that is,
but yours.

I found your hands
in a sink full of suds,
washing nothing
but a hurricane lamp
you found too dirty
atop my counter.
Your hands spoke the words
I have heard a whole lifetime.

I swallowed these words
till they settled like poison
in a hollow deep in my head,
till your rough voice
turned to an echo,
and I took over
the battering.

From you I learned
one lesson too well;
I still haven't learned
to clean house.

Love and Fear

Growing up,
we found it easier to fear
than to love our father,
but that's the way
he favored it.

To look at him now,
red-faced, white-haired, wheezy,
you'd never guess
he was once a Marine,
but the leatherneck will still emerge.
He points at my brother's
rambunctious puppy and declares,
"Dogs are just like children;
all they need is discipline."

Ironically, this puppy is a beagle,
like those we had as kids,
only this wild thing won't cower.
It randomly pees on the carpet
and our father quietly fumes
for he longs to clutch its nape
and rub its snout in the urine,
to curse and thrash it
with the incessant fury
of a long black strap
till it whimpers into submission.
We know that strap,
as he held back nothing but love,
repeated in rhythms
on our bare bottoms
as we lurched across his lap
and counted aloud each lash.

Our mother played stoolie,
a willing collaborator
with her habitual threat:
"Wait till your father gets home!"
Then she'd wash her hands of us
as our father, her eager henchman,
worked off his own frustrations.

As a Marine
he'd been trained to kill.
When Holly had puppies
he drowned the whole litter,
only he waited a month
till we had nurtured and named them
before dumping them into a well.
We knew we too could end up
floating like fallen apples
in a dark and stagnant hole,
our abortive squeals unheard.

My drowning story was less dramatic.
On an Ozark vacation,
he pushed me despite his promises
off the end of a metal pier
to force me to learn to swim.
I sputtered, swallowed,
and sank like concrete.
Then he fished me out,
laughing as I labored for breath,
before shoving me back in the deep.

Continued

My stubborn brothers,
even through their teens,
fortified his rage.
They fought back
and refused to shed a tear.
I was never smacked like a puck
with a hockey stick like Mark,
or lifted off the floor like Brad
with a stranglehold around the throat.
My scars were below the surface,
etched in my bones
like scrimshaw;
like the family dogs,
I learned to cower.

We have faced our fears
in predictable adult ways—
Prozac, alcohol, cocaine—
but we no longer fear our father.
Now we fear becoming him.

Empty Nest

The impatient wait is over.
Our house is now our own.

No more rap music
scratching at doors in the morning.
No more coming home
to a house lit up like a runway.
No more demanding notes
dangling from ceiling fans,
or trails of trash
left like Gretel's breadcrumbs.

No more hair dye
blacking the bathtub.
Bye-bye to black light posters.
And his black bedroom walls
can at last be painted bright white.

I can make coffee
in the kitchen in the nude.
We can kiss on the sofa
without comments or groans.
We can make love
with the bedroom door open,
and we don't have to muffle
the sounds of our pleasure.

It took a year,
but your son's finally
done something that pleases me.

Photograph

This is the way
you wanted to be remembered.

Elegant black dress,
sophisticated white pearls,
a radiant halo of hair,
blond as Marilyn Monroe's.
Contacts, green as hundred dollar bills,
that draw men to your eyes.
Perpetually tanned, too,
like a Fifties' movie star.
This photograph is more
head shot for Hollywood
than portrait for an obituary.

Sometimes we get the chance
to realize our dreams
before we lose touch with life.
We journey to Borneo,
purchase a Porsche,
or hang-glide off a cliff.
You prepared for death
by perfecting your image,
becoming your own press agent.
What were we to think,
when you handed us
the 8 x 10 color glossies?
All they were missing
was an autograph—
and any hint of cancer.

Despite your best orchestrations,
I will remember you
the way I have known you—
more Norma Jean than icon,
less distant, more mother.

TOMATOES

Tomatoes

Things are heating up in the red-light district.

The tomatoes flaunt their pendulous breasts,
exposing their flesh like whores.
They tease, they beckon,
"Let us be your little love-apples!
C'mon, we're ripe for the picking!"

The lecherous old birds are hooked.
They leer, they ogle, they cruise.
They've a taste for something scarlet and cheap.
They'll ravish those juicy trollops.
They'll nibble, they'll prod, they'll poke.

Then they'll slink like sinners homeward,
where they'll prop up their beaks and drink Bloody Marys,
leaving tomatoes in beds
saturated with wet spots,
pulp running down their smug stems.

Moonbathing

A trio of nude young men
lined up like the catch-of-the-day,
deliciously stretched across the deck,
waxing in the moon's full glow.

Their heads are hung low,
chins cast down, prayerlike,
faces hidden in gentle shadow:
resplendent bodies in lunar light.

The arcs of their shoulders
quiver like roosting doves.
Their smooth backs slope to valleys
where trickles of perspiration gleam.

Their posteriors are ivory orbs
split by crescents of darkness,
covered with a breezy down,
an undulating prairie of wheat.

Their legs sublime, solid oars,
ripple across the planks.
Even their soles shine white,
vulnerable, silken, longing.

No madness is reflected;
no baying will be heard.
Yet charmed as sleepy waters
are men who bathe in moonlight.

Titillating

Your nipples pout sumptuously,
like the collagen-injected lips
of rising Hollywood starlets.
But this swelling is real—
teased by fingers into performance,
tempered by a combination of tenderness
and rough-and-tumble desire.
Pinched to the mouth-watering edge
where pleasure's a hairsbreadth from pain,
your nipples, raw as uncut diamonds,
bloom like succulent plums.
When at last daylight retires,
your hard little gems pulse and shine
with enough greed to win an Oscar.

How You Touch Me

Your fingers breathe
    across my sleepy lips,
        down my neck,
mark my morning stubble
with tender fog.

Your hands sing
    over my shoulders
        across my arching chest,
work out warming notes
in fluid arias.

Your tongue pipes
    through my belly's bristle
        down my waking penis,
stirs my name
with its moist frosting.

Your feet whisper
    down my quiet thigh
        over my ankles,
feather my legs
with drowsy arousal.

Your heart shouts
    through my yielding flesh
        to my very core,
echoes in receptive chambers
that answer in absolute yes.

Scrabble

I'd been slightly behind
for most of the game,
till you gave me the opening
that I'd been seeking
when you formed the word
ENNUI with your tiles.

Below your *I*, I slapped my *F*,
followed by a *U*, a *C*,
and on that bright red spot,
beckoning like a target, a *K*:
triple word score,
forty-four delicious points.

"Fuck you," you balked,
but I claimed my move legitimate.
FUCK, I explained,
while invariably brief,
was not an abbreviation,
did not require a hyphen,
was generally not capitalized,
and was hopefully not foreign.

You fumbled through the dictionary,
took your time perusing rules,
then grunted, groaned, and acquiesced.
I won the game without the
satisfaction I had expected,
the last time you let me fuck you.

Playing GI Joes

My GI Joe didn't care for camouflage,
that dreary mélange of green and khaki.
He preferred the minimal clothes that I created
with a pair of scissors and poor sewing skills:
hot little loincloths attached with a pin,
paisley ponchos that required only a hole,
a strip of red velvet for a headband or belt.

My GI Joe craved reconnaissance missions.
He would sneak about my sister's room,
raiding Barbie's boutique for fashion ideas,
trying on faux fur and elastic-banded skirts,
tube tops and a white-beaded bridal veil—
forays which seldom produced good fits
but occasionally spawned fantastic accessories.

My GI Joe was a gung-ho exhibitionist.
He'd rip off his Army fatigue jacket,
metal snaps rat-a-tatting like an M-1 rifle;
he'd strut that smooth plastic chest
as if his twelve-inch stature controlled the barracks;
then he'd drop his pants around the ankles,
displaying buttocks as solid as rocks—
an audacious tease for one without a penis.

My GI Joe learned to take a lot of pain.
He'd volunteer to cross into enemy terrain,
where he'd be captured without a struggle,
stripped like a go-go boy, and thrown into a cell.
Tied up, disciplined, tortured into a frenzy,
he was a master of man-to-man endurance,
revealing only name, rank, and serial number
as a sly grin edged toward the scar on his cheek,
a mark that covered so many of our secrets.

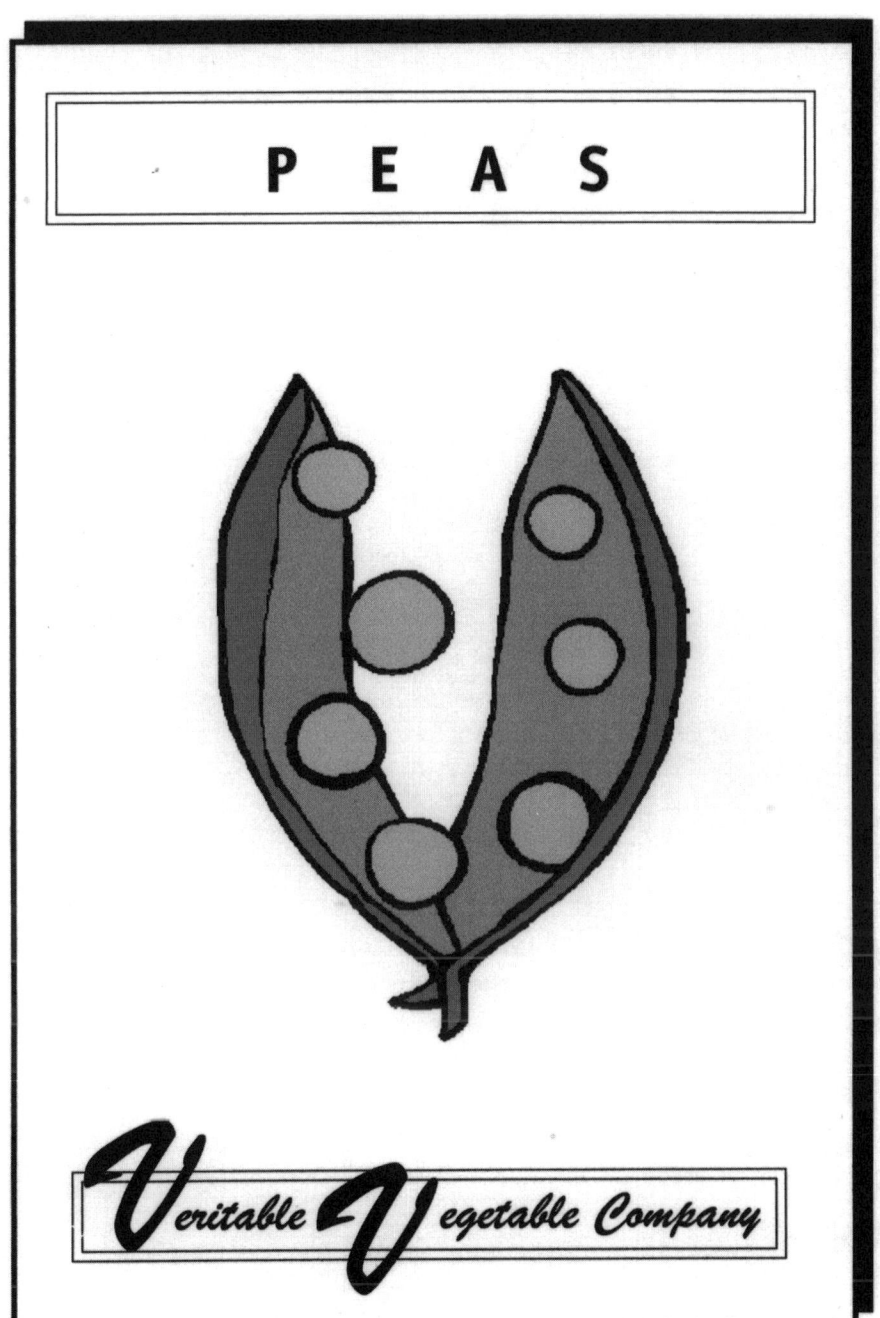

P E A S

Veritable Vegetable Company

Peas

Already they crouch earthward
toward mulch and decaying matter.
Memories flicker through their veins
sporadically, like distant lightning,
though they'd swear that spring was yesterday,
when fresh and lofty they climbed,
green as a forest's velvet carpet.

Already they hear with certainty
the awful rattle in their shells,
the hoary scratch of skin so bleached
it crackles like dried-out leather.
Deceptively delicate yet tenacious as weeds,
their trembling tendrils clutch to the living
with the strength of those damned to die.

Be it man or vegetable,
time is always too fleeting,
death, always undignified.

The Wake

Outside the parlor, crows screeched,
their feathers blackening the landscape.
Inside, the butcher's big hands, silent
as knives, lay clasped on his stomach.

I'd just seen him behind the meat counter,
all bone-white teeth and bloodied apron.
Now, his mouth sewn tight as an inseam,
his suit as unaccustomed as my own.

I stared without horror at my first dead body,
wondering if the flesh would feel like wax,
or like the soot of Ash Wednesday.

His only daughter, a classmate,
cried quietly in the first pew,
and I imagined my own father
still and helpless in the coffin,
my Catholic guilt rising
like an unwanted erection.

I knelt with the others and prayed—
not for the butcher or his daughter,
but for my own stray desires,
squawking as black and loud
as the crows outside.

Cremation

I hadn't noticed your wife
sitting quietly on the other sofa.
Then you introduced me,
and in my arms I took her,
sealed in a plain brown wrapper
like an obscene package
with no return address.

Then I handed back her ashes,
and in your arms you held her,
drifted into a close dance
as loneliness welled in your eyes
and six months of tears
waltzed through your heart.

I wanted to hold you,
and you needed to be held,
but I kept myself from cutting in,
realizing that Margaret was right:
"The last arms to hold you
are always your own."

Nightscape

Pale gardens quiver tonight.
Furtive leaves crouch in closure,
blend to backgrounds like chameleons.
Roses huddle in coils of velvet
and quiet gardenias fold to loam.

I too lie low to the earth,
slither on my belly in dew-covered grass
and catch a sight of the sky.
The moon is cloudy as a cataract;
the night is hidden with you.

Tarot

With you, it was always pomp,
performance, razzle-dazzle:
never halfway, always hyperbole.
You learned to believe
your layers of charades;
then you learned to live them.

Of course, your deck of Russian cards,
wrapped impressively in crimson silk,
was a prop to your high drama.
Swords and cups, wands and pentacles,
positioned on fabric as impeccably as tiles,
then smack in the center the card I drew.
I played into your hands just perfectly,
for Death had become my *significator*.

You always read me wrong.
You saw a shyness in my smile,
not the grimace of gritting teeth.
You saw a quiet in my guise,
not the paralysis of fear.
You saw a gentleness in my eyes,
not the skittish search for flight.

You saw Death as elimination,
as shedding fixed attitudes,
as accepting the inevitable,
which naturally was you.

Death is simply the end.
Your reading was off again.

El Día de los Muertos

My altar's littered
not with sunny marigold petals
nor with festive *papel picado*,
but with lives I chose to bury.

An empty prescription bottle
glistening like burnt sugar
with its suicidal breath:
the end of adolescent life.

A cheap plastic rosary
of powdery black beads
and a paucity of prayers:
the end of religious life.

A ragged pack of rolling papers,
the disposable seeds and stems
of higher learning:
the end of academic life.

A wizened leather glove
lined with the wintry smell
of cold wet wool:
the end of Northern life.

A forsaken wedding band
tarnished with the crust
of unplanned obsolescence:
the end of marital life.

There have been others,
tossed aside like coffee grounds,
interred in the compost of memory.

Mi ofrenda's filled
with long-neglected objects,
smirking like *calaveras*,
each etched with my name.
Many deaths, but only one soul,
a sweet lump of bread
glazed with white bones,
a *pan de muertos* peace offering
to the lives I had to end.

Shape-Shifter

You waste no time. I'll give you that.
While grandmother's hull folds in on itself,
shrivels with tumors and chemicals,
I await the call to fly off to her funeral.

But you couldn't wait for another victim.
You crawled in bed with my youngest brother,
unfurled yourself while he lay dreaming,
and spread your shadow over his esophagus.
They say the way to a man is through his stomach,
but you've perfected every technique;
no organ is exempt from your dark embrace.

When your fingers clasped my mother's throat,
her voice immediately dropped several registers.
Teams of doctors loosened your grasp.
She didn't end up with an artificial voice box,
but I hear your echo when she speaks.

I was the next to escape your clutches,
and you let me off rather painlessly,
a bite on the leg, black as a horsefly.
Not that I haven't taken your visit seriously.
I check my skin with the diligence of a curator;
like you, I'm forced to stay in the shade.

With my father, you attacked the prostate,
spread your scaly fingers up his dark cavity
and pushed down like a rusty piston.
A buckshot of radioactive pellets chased you off;
yet you lurk in the air like a scavenger.
Circling my family in a restless gyration,
you'll be gorging again too soon.

Humus

The garden is in shambles,
like an abandoned gravesite
forgotten in the country.
The brown detritus of decay
falls from spindly stems
to the homes of worms below.
Beneath the drugget of rot,
beneath crumbled leaves
and vegetables' offal,
life in the depths of death
prepares for the rich season
of yet another coming.

About the Author

Scott Wiggerman's career in poetry started modestly in the mid-1990s. A board member of the Austin International Poetry Festival for the past six years, Scott served as the founding editor for the festival's *di-verse-city* anthologies. Now in its fourth year, the *di-verse-city* series exemplifies the high standard Scott established with *di-verse-city* itself (1997), followed by *di-verse-city too* (98) and *très di-verse-city* (99). Currently Poetry Editor for the "Austin Writer," Scott has organized and hosted dozens of poetry readings in and around Austin, including a successful monthly reading for Central Texas gay and lesbian poets.

Scott's first poetry volume, a chapbook entitled "Vegetable Logic," won a Special Citation from the Austin Writers' League's Violet Crown Awards in 1996. His poem "What Poets Are Good For" captured the Poetry Society of Texas award in 1997. A juried poet at the Houston Poetry Fest of 1998, Scott has published widely in respected poetry journals.

Born in North Carolina and raised in the Midwest, Scott found his way to Texas in 1980, as an instructor of English at Southwest Texas State University. Currently a high school librarian, he has sponsored poetry readings and writing workshops in the Austin schools, including a series of Poetry Coffeehouses at McCallum High School that has proved successful with students and faculty alike. An avid proponent of poetry, Scott has merged his dual careers as poet and educator with events such as "A Rhyme in Time: Library Programming with Poets and Poetry," a popular workshop for Austin public school librarians.

Scott lives in central Austin, with his partner David Meischen and their cats, Bullet and Blanca.